FOLLOW THAT FOOD CHAIN

A MANGROVE FOREST Food Chain

A WHO-EATS-WHAT Adventure in Asia

Rebecca Hogue Wojahn   Donald Wojahn

Lerner Publications Company
Minneapolis

For Eli and Cal. We hope this answers some of your questions.

There are many links in the chain that created this series. Thanks to Susan Rose, Carol Hinz, Danielle Carnito, Sarah Olmanson, Paul Rodeen, the staff of the L. E. Phillips Memorial Public Library, and finally, Katherine Hogue

Lerner Publications Company
A division of Lerner Publishing Group, Inc.
241 First Avenue North
Minneapolis, MN 55401 U.S.A.

Website address: www.lernerbooks.com

Library of Congress Cataloging-in-Publication Data

Wojahn, Rebecca Hogue.
   A mangrove forest food chain : a who-eats-what adventure in Asia / by Rebecca Hogue Wojahn and Donald Wojahn.
      p.   cm. — (Follow that food chain)
   Includes bibliographical references and index.
   ISBN 978-0-8225-7615-0 (lib. bdg. : alk. paper)
   1. Mangrove ecology—Asia—Juvenile literature. 2. Food chains (Ecology)—Asia—Juvenile literature. I. Wojahn, Donald. II. Title.
QH541.5.M27W65 2010
577.69'816095—dc22   2008052576

Manufactured in the United States of America
1 2 3 4 5 6 – BP – 15 14 13 12 11 10

FOLLOW THAT FOOD CHAIN

Contents

Introduction
WELCOME TO THE
MANGROVE FOREST

The ocean waves wash ashore on the Southeast Asian island of Borneo. But it's hard to tell exactly where the ocean ends and the island begins. The ocean just gets shallower, and the trees grow right out of the salty water. In this space, between water and solid land, the mangrove forest grows.

Watch your step. The tree roots tangle together in a wild maze that makes exploring the area very tricky. And even though the shade is deep, the air drips with heat and moisture. As you head farther inland, mosquitoes swarm around your sweaty face. The buzz of thousands of cicadas fills your ears. A rotten-egg smell rises up as you step over a clump of dead fern leaves. Here the sound of the ocean finally fades out. But shallow saltwater pools, pockets of mud, and freshwater streams are still found between the stiltlike roots of the trees.

Here in the mangrove forest, many **species** of animals have **adapted** to live both in the water and on the ground. Monkeys swim. Fish scoot around on land. Lobsters dig in the mud. Come meet just a few of these species in this book.

Brunei

South
China
Sea

Sulu
Sea

Pacific
Ocean

Celebes
Sea

MALAYSIA

INDONESIA

Java Sea

Indian
Ocean

Borneo

N

mangrove
forest

Choose a
TERTIARY CONSUMER

All the living things in the mangrove forest are necessary for its health and survival. From the Borneo clouded leopard prowling the water's edge to the porcelain fiddler crab rummaging through the mud, all living things are connected. Some animals feed on other animals. Other animals eat plants. Plants collect energy from the sun and **nutrients** from the soil. Together this is called a **food chain**. Energy is transferred from one member of the chain to another. In every **habitat**, food chains are linked together to become a **food web**.

In a food web, the strongest **predators** are called **tertiary consumers**. They hunt other animals for food and have few natural enemies. Some of the animals they eat are called **secondary consumers**. Secondary consumers are also predators. They hunt plant-eating animals. Plant-eating animals are **primary consumers**.

Plants are **producers**. Using energy from the sun and nutrients from the soil, they produce their own food.

Decomposers are animals or **bacteria** that break down dead plants and animals so their valuable nutrients can be returned to the soil.

The plants and animals in a food web depend on one another. Sometimes there's a break in a chain, such as one type of animal dying out. This loss ripples through the rest of the habitat.

Begin your journey through the mangrove forest food web by choosing a large **carnivore**, or meat eater. These tertiary consumers are at the top of their food chain. That means that as healthy adults, they don't have any enemies in the mangrove forest except for humans.

When it's time for the tertiary consumer to eat, choose its meal and flip to that page. As you go through the book, don't be surprised if you backtrack and end up where you never expected to be. That's how food webs work—they're complicated. And watch out for those dead ends! That's when a species is **endangered** and there aren't enough animals alive to feed another species. When you hit one of these dead ends, go back to page 7 and start over with another tertiary consumer.

The main role a plant or animal plays in the mangrove forest food web is identified by a color-coded shape. Here is the key to that code:

TERTIARY CONSUMER

PRODUCER

SECONDARY CONSUMER

DECOMPOSER

PRIMARY CONSUMER

To choose . . .

. . . an otter civet, TURN TO PAGE 8.

. . . a saltwater crocodile, TURN TO PAGE 9.

. . . a crested serpent eagle, TURN TO PAGE 21.

. . . a Borneo clouded leopard, TURN TO PAGE 29.

. . . an Indian monitor lizard, TURN TO PAGE 43.

To learn more about a mangrove forest food web, GO TO PAGE 34.

OTTER CIVET *(Cynogale bennettii)*

The otter civet watches the water. Only her eyes are visible above the water's surface. This catlike mammal hides her 30-inch-long (76-centimeter), brown-furred body underneath the water.

A frog splashes nearby. The civet glides closer with a push of her webbed feet. As she moves, her ears close up inside so that water can't get in. Her nostrils open upward so that she doesn't breathe in water. She draws closer to the frog. . . .

Unfortunately, not a lot is known about how the otter civet hunts and catches her food. She's secretive and rare. And she's getting rarer. In the last few years, the number of otter civet sightings has dropped by half. Scientists aren't sure how many are left in the wild. Because of this, otter civets are in danger of becoming **extinct**. And because of that, this is a *DEAD END*.

SALTWATER CROCODILE _(Crocodylus porosus)_

The saltwater crocodile lurks at the edge of the forest. At 15 feet (5 meters) long and 800 pounds (360 kilograms), she's the biggest predator of the mangrove forest. She cruises through the water wherever she wants—it doesn't matter if the water is salty or fresh. She can hunt in both.

She rests on the shore, her mouth open wide. As a cold-blooded reptile, her body temperature is the same as the air around her. The breeze blowing through her open mouth helps cool her.

She hasn't picked this spot on the shore randomly. Nearby is her nest of eggs. They are hidden in a shallow mound of earth. Although she is resting and hasn't moved in hours, she's actively guarding her eggs. She watches as a monitor lizard draws near. In an instant, the crocodile lunges forward with a growl, powerful jaws snapping. The monitor lizard shoots away. But the crocodile can move fast. She chases it for a few steps. The monitor lizard just barely escapes.

The crocodile nudges her nest, then settles back down. She's **nocturnal**. Later, as it grows darker, she'll slip into the water for a quick meal.

Last night for dinner, the saltwater crocodile chomped down . . .

10

. . . an otter civet paddling through the mangrove roots. To see what another otter civet is up to, TURN TO PAGE 8.

. . . a Borneo clouded leopard cub that came to the water's edge for a drink. To see what a clouded leopard is up to, TURN TO PAGE 29.

. . . an Oriental small-clawed otter searching for food. To see what another Oriental small-clawed otter is up to, TURN TO PAGE 12.

. . . a dog-faced water snake swimming through the water. To see what another dog-faced water snake is up to, TURN TO PAGE 46.

. . . a Malaysian giant turtle basking in the sun, swallowed whole. To see what another Malaysian giant turtle is up to, TURN TO PAGE 16.

. . . a common kingfisher bird, snatched from its perch on a low branch. To see what another common kingfisher is up to, TURN TO PAGE 48.

. . . a young crested serpent eagle out for its first hunt. To see what another crested serpent eagle is up to, TURN TO PAGE 21.

ORIENTAL SMALL-CLAWED OTTER

(Aonyx cinerea)

The Oriental small-clawed otter dives under the water. As she does, her nose and ears seal off so water doesn't get in them. She explores underwater. She has very short claws at the ends of her paws. The claws are almost like fingers, letting her poke around the cracks and crevices of the stones.

Aha! Her paw closes around a shellfish. She swims to the shore with it. As she adds the shellfish to a pile in the sun, her younger brother noses it. She pushes him off. She's over a year older than he is, and she teaches him a lot. The shellfish will open up on its own if it is left in the sun for a while. It's much easier than trying to crack the shell.

Her younger brother chases her back into the water. They play chase and tag, darting around in the shallow water. After a while, their parents and siblings join in. As they play, they chatter and grunt at one another.

One by one, the otters grow tired of the game and head back to the nest. Their father adds fresh leaves to their family nest. For the rest of the afternoon, the otters take turns resting in the sun and grooming one another.

Finally, it's time to eat. The shellfish in the pile have opened. Slurp! Their soft insides slide right down the otters' throats.

Last night for dinner, the Oriental small-clawed otter ate . . .

. . . **a giant mudskipper skipping along the sand.** To see what another giant mudskipper is up to, TURN TO PAGE 26.

. . . **a porcelain fiddler crab dug out of the sand.** To see what another porcelain fiddler crab is up to, TURN TO PAGE 51.

. . . **a scorpion mud lobster hiding under a rock.** To see what another scorpion mud lobster is up to, TURN TO PAGE 32.

. . . **a crab-eating frog that hopped a little too near the otters' home.** To see what another crab-eating frog is up to, TURN TO PAGE 54.

. . . **an archerfish caught during an underwater dive.** To see what another archerfish is up to, TURN TO PAGE 41.

MANGROVE APPLE *(Sonneratia alba)*

Some of the trees in the mangrove forest are mangrove apples. They crowd near the shore. Some of the mangrove apple's roots go down deep into the water and ground. But so much water is in the soil that the tree can't get nutrients from it. So mangrove apples have developed "breathing roots." Breathing roots are knobby root ends that stick up out of the mud and water. They allow a mangrove more access to the air. But all those knobby roots make the mangrove forest difficult for humans to explore.

As the day grows dimmer, the mangrove apple's white spiky blossoms start to open. Insects and bats flit around. Each of these blossoms will last only one night. By dawn they'll fall off the tree. But more open each night to feed the **nocturnal** creatures of the mangrove forest.

Last night for dinner, the mangrove apple trees soaked up nutrients from . . .

Above: The blossom of a mangrove apple opens at night.
Left: The roots of the mangrove apple stick up like spikes.

. . . a decomposing large flying fox. To see what another large flying fox is up to, TURN TO PAGE 17.

. . . dead weaver ants. To see what other weaver ants are up to, TURN TO PAGE 35.

. . . a decomposing crested serpent eagle egg. To see what a crested serpent eagle is up to, TURN TO PAGE 21.

. . . the soil dug up by a porcelain fiddler crab. To see what a porcelain fiddler crab is up to, TURN TO PAGE 51.

. . . the soil dug up by a scorpion mud lobster. To see what a scorpion mud lobster is up to, TURN TO PAGE 32.

. . . a decomposing long-tailed macaque. To see what another long-tailed macaque is up to, TURN TO PAGE 56.

MALAYSIAN GIANT TURTLE (*Orlitia borneensis*)

The Malaysian giant turtle scoots through the murky water. He spies the silver flash of a fish ahead of him. He shoots forward and latches onto the fish with his hooked mouth. He gulps the fish down, but he can't quite swallow it.

Before he knows it, the turtle is being jerked up through the water. The fish he swallowed was bait. The hook has stuck in his throat, and the turtle is being hauled aboard a boat. He won't be returning to the mangrove forest. This is a **DEAD END**. Malaysian giant turtles are endangered because humans have killed too many of them.

Smuggled Away

Despite being protected by hunting laws, Malaysian giant turtles are often smuggled out of the mangrove forests of Borneo to be sold illegally. This turtle might turn up somewhere in Asia as someone's dinner. He might be caught so his shell can be ground up and sold as medicine—some people believe turtle shells have healing properties. Or he might be shipped across the ocean to be sold as a pet. Because of illegal sales, these turtles are becoming increasingly scarce.

LARGE FLYING FOX
(Pteropus vampyrus)

As the sky darkens over the forest, large flying fox bats stretch out their huge wings under the branches of the trees. The **colony** of bats is restless. The bats are ready to take off for their nightly feeding. One by one, the bats swoop out from under the trees. Their number and the size of their wings—nearly 5 feet (1.5 meters) across—almost block out the night sky. They head inland as a group.

Despite their size, these bats are harmless to other animals. They eat the fruit, the nectar, and the blossoms of the swamp.

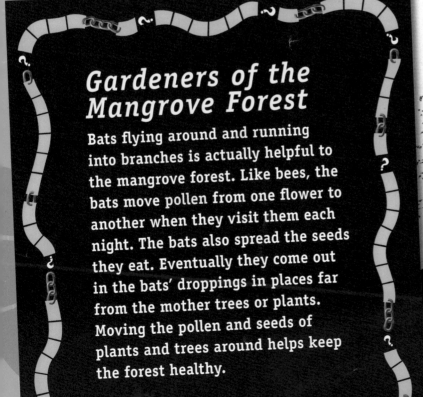

17

Gardeners of the Mangrove Forest

Bats flying around and running into branches is actually helpful to the mangrove forest. Like bees, the bats move pollen from one flower to another when they visit them each night. The bats also spread the seeds they eat. Eventually they come out in the bats' droppings in places far from the mother trees or plants. Moving the pollen and seeds of plants and trees around helps keep the forest healthy.

One female flying fox hones in on a particularly fruitful branch of a tree. Unlike most other bats, she doesn't use sound waves to find her food. She smells it and sees it. As she nears the branch, she doesn't have a graceful way to grab her food. She just runs into the branch.

Twigs and leaves shower to the ground. Then, swoop, the bat hooks her feet around the main branch and swings upside down. She's ready to start pulling fruit to her mouth with her thumbs, the hooks at the top edge of her wings.

Last night for dinner, the large flying fox ate . . .

18

. . . flowers from a mangrove apple tree. To see what the mangrove apples are like, **TURN TO PAGE 14.**

. . . seeds from api api putih trees. To see what the api api putih are like, **TURN TO PAGE 38.**

GOSSAMER-WINGED BUTTERFLIES

(Lycaenidae family)

A gossamer-winged butterfly caterpillar wriggles her way up the twig. Hordes of weaver ants stream around her. Normally, they devour any insect in their path, but they don't bother the caterpillar. In fact, they've been taking care of her. When she was newly hatched, the ants brought her into their leaf nest to feed. And when she molted, they carried her outside to rest and feed on the best leaves. They push and prod her every ten minutes or so to "milk" her. The caterpillar squeezes out a sweet liquid called honeydew that the ants eat.

Weaver ants milk a gossamer-winged butterfly caterpillar for its honeydew.

Friends or Enemies?

There are many different types of gossamer-winged butterflies. Not all of them are so helpful to the ants. Some species have adapted to take advantage of the ants. Once the ants bring them into their nest, the caterpillars turn on the ants. They eat the ant

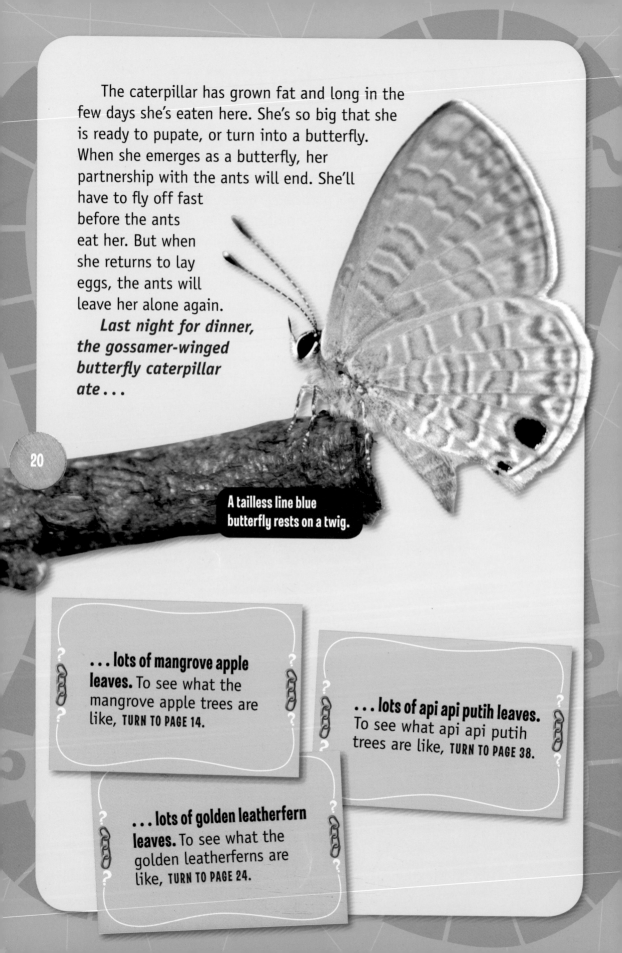

The caterpillar has grown fat and long in the few days she's eaten here. She's so big that she is ready to pupate, or turn into a butterfly. When she emerges as a butterfly, her partnership with the ants will end. She'll have to fly off fast before the ants eat her. But when she returns to lay eggs, the ants will leave her alone again.

Last night for dinner, the gossamer-winged butterfly caterpillar ate . . .

A tailless line blue butterfly rests on a twig.

20

. . . lots of mangrove apple leaves. To see what the mangrove apple trees are like, **TURN TO PAGE 14.**

. . . lots of api api putih leaves. To see what api api putih trees are like, **TURN TO PAGE 38.**

. . . lots of golden leatherfern leaves. To see what the golden leatherferns are like, **TURN TO PAGE 24.**

CRESTED SERPENT EAGLE (*Spilornis cheela*)

The young crested serpent eagle hops about in her nest. Up here in the treetops, the sun is bright and she's uncomfortable. She can hear her parents call as they soar up above the forest. *Keee-keeee-ke!* When will they come back to her?

She hops to the edge of the 2-foot-wide (0.6-meter) stick nest. It hangs above a marshy river. The eagle chick peers over. But she's not ready to fly yet. She'll just have to wait for her parents' return. Crested serpent eagles lay only one egg each year, so at least the chick won't have to share whatever her parents bring back.

A baby crested serpent eagle waits in its nest.

Top: A crested serpent eagle tends to its chick.
Bottom: A crested serpent eagle scans for its next meal.

With a swoosh, her parents flap in. The eagle's father has brought a snake. It still wriggles in his curved beak. Eagerly, the chick takes it. Meanwhile, the mother eagle stretches her wings out around the eagle chick. She'll block the sun for her chick through the hottest hours of the day. The eagle parents do all they can to keep the chick safe. Still, the odds aren't in the chick's favor. Out of every four crested serpent eagle chicks, three won't live to adulthood. But this young eagle is healthy and strong. She may just make it.

Last night for dinner, the crested serpent eagle ate . . .

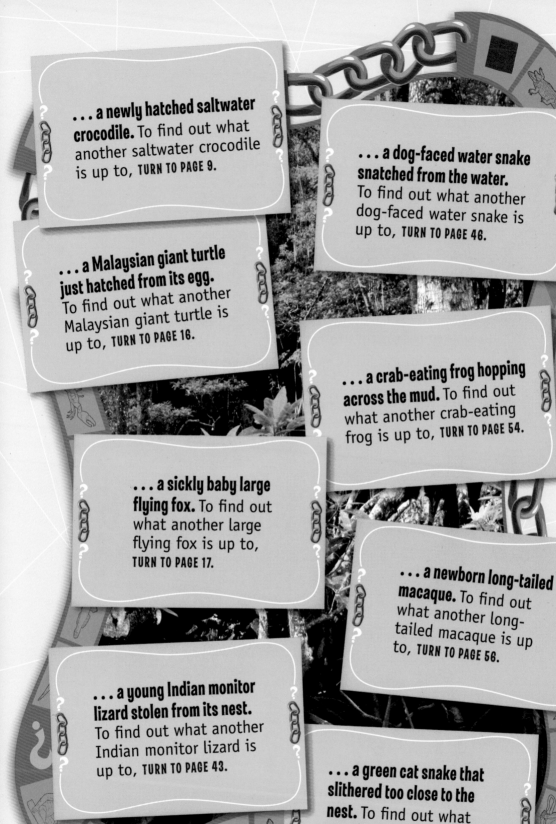

. . . **a newly hatched saltwater crocodile.** To find out what another saltwater crocodile is up to, TURN TO PAGE 9.

. . . **a dog-faced water snake snatched from the water.** To find out what another dog-faced water snake is up to, TURN TO PAGE 46.

. . . **a Malaysian giant turtle just hatched from its egg.** To find out what another Malaysian giant turtle is up to, TURN TO PAGE 16.

. . . **a crab-eating frog hopping across the mud.** To find out what another crab-eating frog is up to, TURN TO PAGE 54.

. . . **a sickly baby large flying fox.** To find out what another large flying fox is up to, TURN TO PAGE 17.

. . . **a newborn long-tailed macaque.** To find out what another long-tailed macaque is up to, TURN TO PAGE 56.

. . . **a young Indian monitor lizard stolen from its nest.** To find out what another Indian monitor lizard is up to, TURN TO PAGE 43.

. . . **a green cat snake that slithered too close to the nest.** To find out what another green cat snake is up to, TURN TO PAGE 58.

GOLDEN LEATHERFERN *(Acrostichum aureum)*

As you get farther inland from the ocean, the plants under the mangroves start to grow thicker. In some places, golden leatherferns sprout up, filling in the spaces between the trees. There are no flowers or fruits on them, just clumps of long, feathery leaves as tall as a grown man.

These ferns grow thick, providing shade and shelter for the animals of the mangrove forest. These ferns even help to shade new plants. But sometimes this can backfire. When the mangroves are cut down, sometimes the golden leatherferns grow so well that they don't allow any other plants to take root. Then they are considered a pest. But in the natural order of the mangrove forest, the ferns are welcome spots of shade.

Last night for dinner, the leatherferns soaked up nutrients from . . .

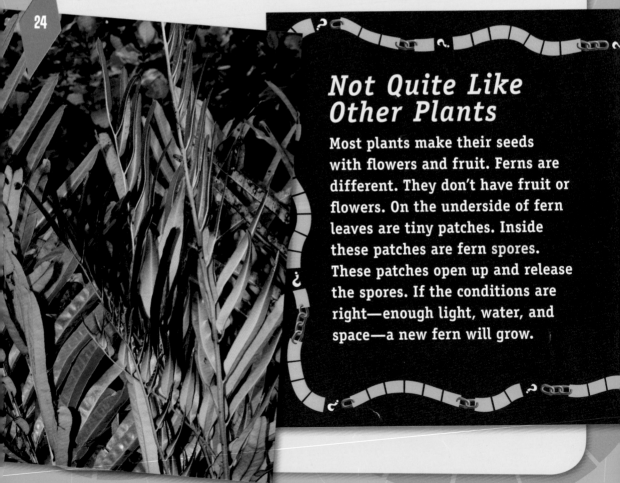

Not Quite Like Other Plants

Most plants make their seeds with flowers and fruit. Ferns are different. They don't have fruit or flowers. On the underside of fern leaves are tiny patches. Inside these patches are fern spores. These patches open up and release the spores. If the conditions are right—enough light, water, and space—a new fern will grow.

. . . a dead gossamer-winged butterfly. To see what another gossamer-winged butterfly is up to, TURN TO PAGE 19.

. . . a rotten Indian monitor lizard egg. To see what an Indian monitor lizard is up to, TURN TO PAGE 43.

. . . a decomposing giant mudskipper. To see what another giant mudskipper is up to, TURN TO PAGE 26.

. . . the soil dug up by a scorpion mud lobster. To see what a scorpion mud lobster is up to, TURN TO PAGE 32.

. . . the soil dug up by a porcelain fiddler crab. To see what a porcelain fiddler crab is up to, TURN TO PAGE 51.

. . . a decomposing green cat snake. To see what another green cat snake is up to, TURN TO PAGE 58.

GIANT MUDSKIPPER *(Periophthalmodon schlosseri)*

A few hours ago, this stretch of beach was underwater. But the tide is going out and the water is creeping back, exposing a widening belt of mud and sand. When there's just 1 inch (2.5 centimeters) or so of water, a strange fish crawls out of his mud burrow and hops across the mud on his front fins. It's a mudskipper. He dug the 20-inch-deep (50 cm) burrow one mouthful of mud at a time.

The mudskipper and his mate push and prod the mud around the burrow with his front fins and her mouth. Soon a low wall circles the burrow entrance. It's a playpen of sorts for their young.

When the tide is all the way out, the young fish crawl out of the burrow. They splash in the muddy water that's trapped by the wall. Like their parents, they can survive in the air, so it doesn't matter if there's not much water.

But look out! On the other side of the wall, another mudskipper creeps toward them. He's hungry for dinner. And young mudskippers look like an easy meal.

A giant mudskipper digs its burrow one mouthful at a time.

The intruding mudskipper draws closer. He braces himself on his two front fins—like crutches—and pushes himself forward.

Just in time, the father mudskipper spies him with his huge bubble eyes. He heaves himself over the edge of the wall. The fin on his back is pointing straight up in alarm. The father launches himself at the intruding mudskipper. The intruder is bigger, and he swipes the father with his front fin. The father mudskipper charges again. The two fish scuffle in the mud, rolling around and snapping at each other.

Meanwhile, the young mudskippers scamper back into their burrow. There they'll be safe. In a little while, their father will return with a mouthful of air for them to breathe underground.

Last night for dinner, the giant mudskipper gobbled down...

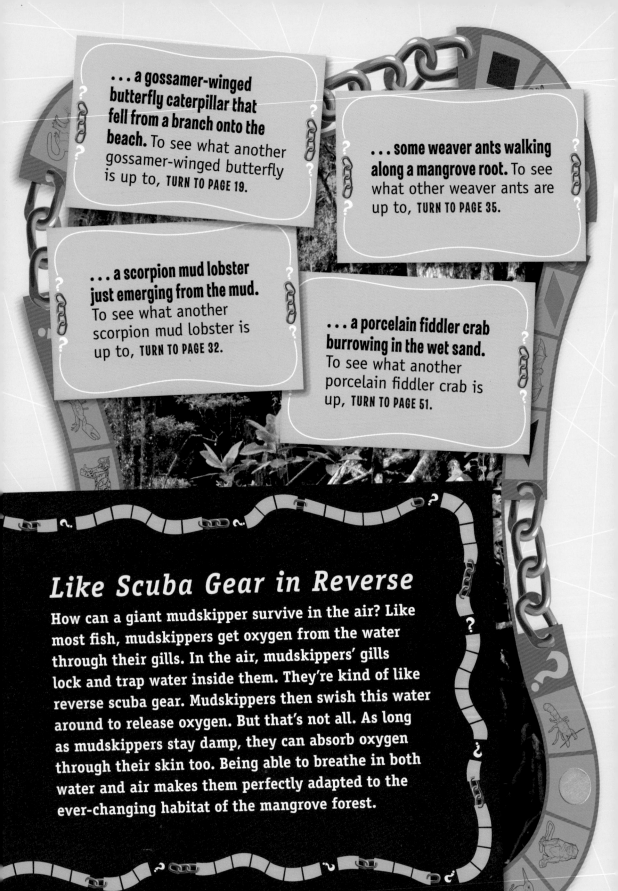

. . . a gossamer-winged butterfly caterpillar that fell from a branch onto the beach. To see what another gossamer-winged butterfly is up to, TURN TO PAGE 19.

. . . some weaver ants walking along a mangrove root. To see what other weaver ants are up to, TURN TO PAGE 35.

. . . a scorpion mud lobster just emerging from the mud. To see what another scorpion mud lobster is up to, TURN TO PAGE 32.

. . . a porcelain fiddler crab burrowing in the wet sand. To see what another porcelain fiddler crab is up, TURN TO PAGE 51.

Like Scuba Gear in Reverse

How can a giant mudskipper survive in the air? Like most fish, mudskippers get oxygen from the water through their gills. In the air, mudskippers' gills lock and trap water inside them. They're kind of like reverse scuba gear. Mudskippers then swish this water around to release oxygen. But that's not all. As long as mudskippers stay damp, they can absorb oxygen through their skin too. Being able to breathe in both water and air makes them perfectly adapted to the ever-changing habitat of the mangrove forest.

BORNEO CLOUDED LEOPARD

(Neofelis nebulosa diardi)

The 3-foot-long (1-meter) Borneo clouded leopard crouches in the treetop. His keen eyes narrow. He has detected a wild pig rooting around the trunk of the tree. As the pig snuffles and snorts along, the leopard follows silently from above. His wide paws balance him perfectly on the bouncy branches.

A New Clouded Leopard

Scientists have been studying clouded leopards on Borneo for at least 100 years. But it wasn't until 2007 that they discovered these leopards are really a different species. Among other differences, the coats of Borneo clouded leopards are unlike the coats of other clouded leopards. Scientists think these leopards came to Borneo about 1.4 million years ago and adapted separately.

29

Mystery Hunter

Clouded leopards are very secretive. No one knows for sure how they hunt. Some people think that they hunt from trees like the leopard in our story. But others think they must pounce on prey from the ground. Most scientists agree that it's probably a combination of both—and that we need to learn more about these mysterious cats.

The leopard sees his opportunity. Slowly, he creeps down the tree trunk headfirst, like a squirrel. He can even hang upside down if he needs to. Most big cats can't do this. But the clouded leopard is made for tricks like these. His anklebones rotate in ways that most cats' anklebones don't. His long claws pierce the bark. His extra-long tail helps him balance.

When the leopard is about 3 feet (1 m) from the pig, the pig looks up and squeals. But it's too late. The leopard leaps, landing on the back of the pig. Clouded leopards have the longest canine teeth of any cat. They are 2 inches (5 centimeters) long, the same size as the much larger tiger. One killing bite from these teeth and it's all over for the pig. The leopard has his dinner.

The Borneo clouded leopard may not eat every day. *Last time he ate, he gorged on . . .*

. . . **an otter civet crawling up a tree trunk.** To see what another otter civet is up to, TURN TO PAGE 8.

. . . **a proboscis monkey baby that wandered too far from its troop.** To see what another proboscis monkey is up to, TURN TO PAGE 50.

. . . **an Oriental small-clawed otter sunning itself on the bank.** To see what another Oriental small-clawed otter is up to, TURN TO PAGE 12.

. . . **a long-tailed macaque swinging through the trees.** To see what another long-tailed macaque is up to, TURN TO PAGE 56.

. . . **a young crested serpent eagle that is just learning to fly.** To see what another crested serpent eagle chick is up to, TURN TO PAGE 21.

. . . **a green cat snake basking on a branch.** To see what another green cat snake is up to, TURN TO PAGE 58.

. . . **an Indian monitor lizard scratching in the dirt.** To see what another Indian monitor lizard is up to, TURN TO PAGE 43.

SCORPION MUD LOBSTER (*Thalassina anomala*)

Several feet under the muddy, sandy surface of the beach, the 6-inch-long (15-centimeter) scorpion mud lobster uses his claws to dig and dig. He's tunneling through the packed mud. He's a decomposer. As he digs, he brings air into the soil. This helps the old, dead bits of plants and animals to decay more quickly. As they decay, they release their precious nutrients back into the soil, where plants can use them.

The mud lobster pushes mud and sand up behind him. A volcano-like mound towers over his burrow. It's almost 2 feet (0.6 meters) tall! The older parts of it are dry and pocked with holes. Lots of creatures have found it the perfect place to live. A **colony** of ants has created a nest, and two spiders call it home. Deep inside, a mud shrimp has his burrow.

Downhill from the mound, other animals gain from the mud lobster's digging too. Mudskippers and crabs splash in the shallow pool that the mud lobster's burrow has created. This is a safe place for them to be during low tide. Meanwhile, the scorpion mud lobster digs out a new tunnel. He isn't seen out in the open very often.

Last night for dinner, the scorpion mud lobster sucked down tiny bits and pieces of...

Digging in the Dirt

The mangrove forest depends on scorpion mud lobsters to stay healthy. Not only do lots of animals find shelter because of the mud lobsters' digging, but mud lobsters also help the plants. By digging through the soil, the mud lobster brings air back into the soil so decomposition can happen. Mud lobsters loosen up the soil so that the seeds of the trees and plants can settle in and grow.

. . . a dead Indian monitor lizard. To see what another Indian monitor lizard is up to, TURN TO PAGE 43.

. . . a dead otter civet. To see what another otter civet is up to, TURN TO PAGE 8.

. . . a decomposing dog-faced water snake. To see what another dog-faced water snake is up to, TURN TO PAGE 46.

. . . a dead Malaysian giant turtle. To see what another Malaysian giant turtle is up to, TURN TO PAGE 16.

. . . a dead proboscis monkey. To see what another proboscis monkey is up to, TURN TO PAGE 50.

. . . a decomposing crested serpent eagle. To see what another crested serpent eagle is up to, TURN TO PAGE 21.

. . . a decaying archerfish. To see what another archerfish is up to, TURN TO PAGE 41.

. . . a decaying green cat snake. To see what another green cat snake is up to, TURN TO PAGE 58.

A MANGROVE FOREST FOOD WEB

In the mangrove forest, energy moves around the food chain from the sun to plants, from plants to plant eaters, and from animals to the creatures that eat them.

WEAVER ANT
(Oecophylla smaragdina)

A weaver ant trots down a twig. Behind her, thousands of other ants spill out of the nest made of leaves. This nest is just one part of the ants' **colony**. The colony has almost a hundred nests like this one in the nearby trees. All the ants are working together. They serve their queen ant, tucked deep inside one of the nests, laying eggs.

The major worker ant's job is to explore new places to add to the colony. Behind her, she leaves a trail of invisible chemicals called **pheromones**. This will help her coworkers follow her.

She approaches a leaf. She tugs at the edge of it, trying to fold it over. Another ant joins her. Soon one hundred ants are pulling and folding the stiff leaf. They line up the leaf so that it meets the leaf above it on the branch. But just as the two edges meet—boing! A long-tailed macaque that is passing through jumps on the branch. The jarring of his landing shakes the ants loose. The leaf springs back in place. The ant finds herself sailing through the air!

The ant lands on a branch below. She scrambles around before she finds old pheromone trails from other ants. She traces her way back up the trunk to the same leaf. Already other ants are pulling the leaves back together again. This time, the leaves are farther apart. That doesn't stop the ants. They link together, creating a chain, and slowly pull the leaves so that they are touching again.

This time nothing interrupts them. While hundreds of ants hold the leaves together, others take off for the nearest nest. They return with white bundles—ant **larvas**—held in their jaws. The larvas squirt out white silk threads that the ants use to bind the leaves together. Once they complete one side, they work on pulling other leaves together. By the end of the day, they'll have a new football-sized nest to add to the colony.

36

Weaver ants use an ant larva to produce silk thread to sew leaves together.

Exploring and building nests isn't the worker ant's only job. She also has to help feed the colony. Once the nest construction is under way and not as many ants are needed, she sets out to hunt with some other worker ants. They scout for other insects to kill and eat.

Ants don't eat tree leaves, but ant colonies depend on trees for their survival. *To learn more about . . .*

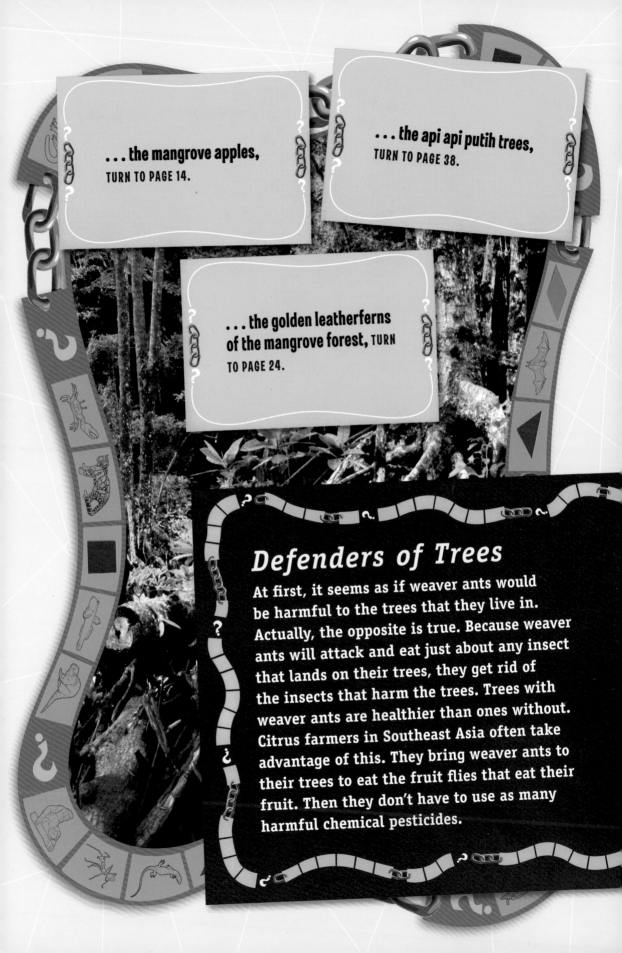

. . . the mangrove apples, TURN TO PAGE 14.

. . . the api api putih trees, TURN TO PAGE 38.

. . . the golden leatherferns of the mangrove forest, TURN TO PAGE 24.

Defenders of Trees

At first, it seems as if weaver ants would be harmful to the trees that they live in. Actually, the opposite is true. Because weaver ants will attack and eat just about any insect that lands on their trees, they get rid of the insects that harm the trees. Trees with weaver ants are healthier than ones without. Citrus farmers in Southeast Asia often take advantage of this. They bring weaver ants to their trees to eat the fruit flies that eat their fruit. Then they don't have to use as many harmful chemical pesticides.

API API PUTIH *(Avicennia alba)*

api api putih leaves

The api api putih are found at the ocean's edge. In some places, these mangrove trees look as if they are wading right into the ocean. Their roots arch over the water and spread wide, giving the trees a good foothold as the tide rushes between them. Most plants and trees would die from the salty ocean. Not the api api putih.

sunlight

carbon dioxide

oxygen

Plants make food and oxygen through photosynthesis. Plants draw in carbon dioxide (a gas found in air) and water. Then they use the energy from sunlight to turn the carbon dioxide and water into their food.

They soak up so much salt from the ocean that their sap tastes salty. Sometimes even their leaves have a salty coating on them.

From the tiny yellow flowers in the treetops to the maze of roots, the api api putih provide food and shelter to the creatures of the mangrove forest. Proboscis monkeys swing in the treetops. Fish hide between their roots. More important, the api api putih protect the land and the sea. They are an important barrier between the two. Without the api api putih and other mangroves, the land would **erode** into the ocean. **Sediments** and pollution from the land would carry out to sea and kill the coral reefs. That's why so many people are so concerned about the destruction of the api api putih forests. If they disappear, there will be far-reaching consequences.

Last night for dinner, the api api putih soaked up nutrients from . . .

Vanishing Forests

If mangrove forests are so important to the health of animal species as well as to the land and ocean, why are they being cut down? Well, for a lot of reasons. Some people want to live on the land. They clear the beachfront of trees. Others clear land so that they can grow crops on the land or in the ocean. Still others cut down the mangroves for their wood. Mangrove wood is used for building and

. . . a decomposing common kingfisher. To see what another common kingfisher is up to, **TURN TO PAGE 48.**

. . . a decomposing saltwater crocodile. To see what another saltwater crocodile is up to, **TURN TO PAGE 9.**

. . . the soil dug up by a scorpion mud lobster. To see what the scorpion mud lobster is up to, **TURN TO PAGE 32.**

. . . the soil dug up by a porcelain fiddler crab. To see what the porcelain fiddler crab is up to, **TURN TO PAGE 51.**

. . . decaying archerfish eggs. To see what an archerfish is up to, **TURN TO PAGE 41.**

. . . a dead crab-eating frog. To see what another crab-eating frog is up to, **TURN TO PAGE 54.**

ARCHERFISH *(Toxotes chatareus)*

An archerfish swims through the **brackish** water where the river flows out to the sea. Several other archerfish swim with him. They gather in a school, heading to the shallows, where the mangrove trees root and branches hang over the water. It's their favorite hunting grounds.

The archerfish uses his large eyes to watch the roots above. The school swirls around a mossy root. A tiny lizard crawls on top of it. The lizard is unaware of the danger below. The archerfish, with their narrow, dark backs, look like shadows on the water from above.

The archerfish draws water into his mouth. He uses his tongue to settle the water into a special groove on the top of his mouth. Then he raises his lips to the surfaces of the water. He clenches his gills shut and—*pow*! A jet of water shoots out of his mouth. It hits the lizard right on the side. Bull's-eye!

The lizard teeters but doesn't fall. More archerfish start shooting. The lizard wobbles and falls off the root. The archerfish jumps and opens his wide mouth to catch the lizard. But he falls back to the water with an empty mouth. Another fish snagged the lizard.

The archerfish swims on. A slug crawls on the edge of a leaf. The archerfish moves underneath it. He can shoot water up to 5 feet (1.5 meters) away, but he's most accurate if he's directly under his **prey**. But before he can aim, another archerfish leaps out of the water and gulps down the slug. If the first archerfish doesn't get a little faster, he may go hungry today.

While the rest of the school heads out to deeper water, the archerfish turns back. He spies a moth fluttering on a leaf. He aims. He shoots. The moth clings to the leaf, but its wings are wet. When the moth tries to fly off, it falls to the water below. The archerfish is waiting. He gulps it down whole.

Last night for dinner, the archerfish shot down and ate . . .

42

. . . **a gossamer-winged butterfly that flew too close to the water's surface.** To find out what another gossamer-winged butterfly is up to, TURN TO PAGE 19.

. . . **a weaver ant that lost its grip on a leaf above.** To find out what other weaver ants are up to, TURN TO PAGE 35.

INDIAN MONITOR LIZARD *(Varanus indicus)*

The Indian monitor lizard pauses halfway up the trunk of the tree. He digs his sharp claws into the bark. What is that smell? He flicks his forked tongue in and out, in and out. The lizard learns about the world through his strong sense of smell, and it's his tongue that picks up the odors around him.

Following the smell, the Indian monitor lizard climbs back down the tree and slips into the water. His long body snakes back and forth as he swims. Farther up the river, he finds what he is looking for. The body of a dead saltwater crocodile sprawls on the bank of the river.

The lizard's approach scares off the birds already feasting on the crocodile. If the lizard wanted to, he could swallow a bird whole. Like many snakes, he can unhinge his jaw to swallow extra-large **prey**.

But the dead crocodile is a much easier meal. The monitor lizard is a **scavenger**, an animal that eats dead animals. He uses his razor-sharp teeth to pull off a hunk of meat. Each of his teeth has jagged edges to help him rip his food apart. He gulps down a chunk. There's enough to last him for days.

Last night for dinner, the Indian monitor lizard ate . . .

44

. . . **a saltwater crocodile hatchling.** To see what another saltwater crocodile is up to, TURN TO PAGE 9.

. . . **an archerfish trapped in a low tide puddle.** To see what another archerfish is up to, TURN TO PAGE 41.

. . . **a crested serpent eagle egg that fell out of its nest.** To see what a crested serpent eagle is up to, TURN TO PAGE 21.

. . . **a giant mudskipper crawling along the riverbank.** To see what another giant mudskipper is up to, TURN TO PAGE 26.

. . . **a common kingfisher egg stolen from a nest.** To see what a common kingfisher is up to, TURN TO PAGE 48.

. . . **a young long-tailed macaque that strayed too far from his mother.** To see what another long-tailed macaque is up to, TURN TO PAGE 56.

DOG-FACED WATER SNAKE (Cerberus rynchops)

As the light of the day grows dim, the dog-faced water snake untangles herself from the watery roots of the mangrove tree. She ripples her body and winds through the water. Like a crocodile's, her eyes and nose are at the top of her head. When she swims, her nose and eyes stay above the water's surface so she can see and breathe. But the rest of her 2-foot-long (0.6-meter) body stays hidden beneath the surface. Her nostrils seal off as a wave washes over her, but her large lungs are full of air. They help keep her body afloat in the shallow water.

The dog-faced water snake curls around the edge of a broken branch in the water. It bobs in the waves. With her brown markings, the snake looks just like a part of the branch. And that's her plan.

A school of archerfish approach. They like the safety of the branch. Slowly, the snake starts wiggling the skinny tip of her tail. One of the fish stops to look. What is that? A worm? A caterpillar that's fallen in the water? The fish creeps closer to investigate.

A dog-faced water snake eats a fish.

Once the fish is in range, the snake snaps her jaws around it. The fangs in the back of her mouth pump **venom** into it. It's not very strong venom, but it does the trick. In a few minutes, the fish is swallowed whole.

Last night for dinner, the dog-faced water snake gobbled up...

. . . **a giant mudskipper.** To see what another giant mudskipper is up to, TURN TO PAGE 26.

. . . **a porcelain fiddler crab wrestling with another crab.** To see what a porcelain fiddler crab is up to, TURN TO PAGE 51.

. . . **a scorpion mud lobster rooting around in the shallow water.** To see what another scorpion mud lobster is up to, TURN TO PAGE 32.

. . . **a crab-eating frog that just laid her eggs.** To see what another crab-eating frog is up to, TURN TO PAGE 54.

. . . **an archerfish swimming through the shallows.** To see what another archerfish is up to, TURN TO PAGE 41.

COMMON KINGFISHER (Alcedo atthis)

Zip! A common kingfisher streaks by in a blue blur. The 6-inch-long (15-centimeter) shimmering blue bird is zooming home with a tiny fish speared in his long, sharp beak. He flits to a high spot in the shore and ducks inside a hole.

It's his nest. Inside are his mate and his brood of four young kingfishers. The chicks hop excitedly. The kingfisher flips the fish around so his beak pinches its tail. Then he tucks it in one of his chicks' wide-open mouth. She swallows the fish down headfirst. It's the kingfisher's turn to eat. He lights out again and heads directly to his favorite perch. He peers into the water. His eyes are perfectly adapted to avoid the glare from the sun and to adjust to seeing things underwater. The kingfisher waits and watches. Then—*pow*! He plunges into the water, snatches a fish, and pops back out. He carries the wriggling fish to his perch. He grabs its tail and slams the fish on the branch a few times. When it's still, he flips the fish into his own mouth. Later on, he'll throw up the bones. As soon as he swallows, he's off to hunt for more. He eats more than half of his body weight in food each day!

Last night for dinner, the common kingfisher tossed down . . .

48

Habitat Gauge

Common kingfishers can be found near bodies of water throughout Europe and Asia. Scientists watch them carefully. Kingfishers are an important sign of the health of their particular habitat. Kingfishers eat lots and lots of little fish and shellfish. If there are any poisons from pollution in the fish, the poison will build up in the kingfishers and kill them. So if kingfisher populations suddenly drop, that could mean the habitat is in trouble.

. . . an archerfish aiming to knock a cricket into the water. To see what another archerfish is up to, **TURN TO PAGE 41.**

. . . a gossamer-winged butterfly caterpillar. To see what another gossamer-winged butterfly is up to, **TURN TO PAGE 19.**

. . . a porcelain fiddler crab. To find out what another porcelain fiddler crab is up to, **TURN TO PAGE 51.**

. . . a giant mudskipper heading home to its burrow. To see what another giant mudskipper is up to, **TURN TO PAGE 26.**

. . . some weaver ants that explored a little too close to the kingfisher's nest. To see what other weaver ants are up to, **TURN TO PAGE 35.**

. . . a crab-eating frog tadpole. To find out what a crab-eating frog is up to, **TURN TO PAGE 54.**

. . . a scorpion mud lobster poking around under the kingfisher's perch. To see what another scorpion mud lobster is up to, **TURN TO PAGE 32.**

PROBOSCIS MONKEY *(Nasalis larvatus)*

The young proboscis monkey clings to his mother's round tummy. Unlike her face, his is blue and his nose is small and upturned. He'll grow a long, dangling nose as he nears adulthood.

His mother flicks her fingers through his hair, grooming him in the early morning light. The rest of the troop wakes and stirs, joining the monkey and his mother. The group climbs and leaps through the trees. They munch on leaves, flowers, fruit, bark, and the occasional bug.

Suddenly, a loud honk echoes through the air. It's the male of their troop. His long nose is red and sticks straight out as he bellows his warning. Someone's coming!

The mother monkey drops from the branch. Splash! She and the baby land in the river. The baby holds tight to his mother as she and the troop dog-paddle across the river. Their partly webbed feet propel them silently.

Behind them, humans stomp through the swamp where the troop was feeding. They are checking out this part of the forest for a logging company. These trees will soon be cut down. The wood will be sold and the land cleared for farming. This is happening too often in the mangrove forests. So many of the trees are being cut down that proboscis monkeys are having a hard time finding places to live. Without places to live, fewer monkeys are born and fewer survive. That's why they're endangered. And that's why this is a **DEAD END**.

50

PORCELAIN FIDDLER CRAB *(Uca annulipes)*

As the tide goes out, the water draws away from the beach and the burrows of porcelain fiddler crabs. A crab pokes his head out of his burrow. The first thing out are his eyes. Poised on the top of long stalks, they survey the sand. No crab-eating birds, snakes, or lizards are around. The crab creeps out of his hole in the sand. His enormous white fiddler claw is almost as big as his whole body.

Soon side-scurrying fiddler crabs of every color cover the beach. The porcelain fiddler crab gets to work eating right away. With his tiny other claw, he pulls sand to his mouth. Bristles in his mouth brush any algae, fungus, or dead matter off into his mouth. The leftover sand is balled up and discarded in front of his burrow. The bits of food are so tiny that the fiddler crab has to eat nearly constantly. The repeated back-and-forth motion of that small claw behind his large claw is how he got his name. It looks as if he's playing a fiddle.

Another crab comes up, a female. Like all females, she has two small claws. The male crab raises his large claw at her. But before

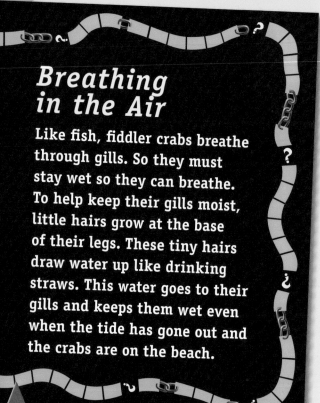

Breathing in the Air

Like fish, fiddler crabs breathe through gills. So they must stay wet so they can breathe. To help keep their gills moist, little hairs grow at the base of their legs. These tiny hairs draw water up like drinking straws. This water goes to their gills and keeps them wet even when the tide has gone out and the crabs are on the beach.

he can get her attention, another male crab pushes his way in, waving his bright orange claw at the porcelain fiddler crab.

The orange-clawed crab pounds his claw on the sand. Then he pushes at the porcelain crab. The porcelain crab shoves back. They don't pinch each other with their claws. Instead, a mini-arm-wrestling match takes place. The female waits patiently as the two males fight.

Suddenly, the orange-clawed crab pins the porcelain crab's claw to the sand. Last week, a kingfisher bird pulled on the claw and injured it. Now it snaps off. That ends the match. The orange-clawed crab takes off with the female.

The porcelain crab steps around his claw and goes back to eating. He'll survive without his fiddler claw. In fact, his smaller claw will grow and become his new fiddler claw.

Last night for dinner, the porcelain fiddler crab nibbled on tiny bits and pieces from . . .

. . . **a decomposing Oriental small-clawed otter.** To see what another Oriental small-clawed otter is like, TURN TO PAGE 12.

. . . **a dead scorpion mud lobster.** To see what another scorpion mud lobster is like, TURN TO PAGE 32.

. . . **a dead archerfish.** To see what another archerfish is like, TURN TO PAGE 41.

. . . **fallen mangrove apple leaves.** To see what the mangrove apples of the forest are like, TURN TO PAGE 14.

. . . **a decomposing common kingfisher.** To see what another common kingfisher is like, TURN TO PAGE 48.

. . . **a decomposing large flying fox.** To see what another large flying fox is like, TURN TO PAGE 17.

. . . **a dead crab-eating frog.** To see what another crab-eating frog is like, TURN TO PAGE 54.

. . . **a dead giant mudskipper.** To see what another giant mudskipper is like, TURN TO PAGE 26.

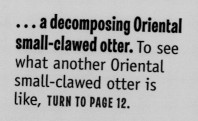

CRAB-EATING FROG *(Fejervarya cancrivora)*

Dodododododok...dododok. The crab-eating frog calls as she crouches in the damp leaves at the edge of the beach. Her call lets other frogs know she is there. She catches a cricket in her wide mouth and crunches it down. Then she stretches out her strong legs and hops out to the water's edge.

Here, at the edge where the fresh river water and the ocean meet, the water is **brackish**. Most **amphibians** would die in the salty seawater. But the salty water doesn't affect the crab-eating frog. Her body has adapted so that it can handle the salt.

The frog glides through the water, coming to rest under a tangle of mangrove roots. Only her eyes and the tip of her nose are visible. She doesn't know it, but she has attracted the attention of something hidden in the leaves.

With a burst of speed, a dog-faced water snake strikes out at the frog. At the last second, the frog dives. She burrows down to safety in the dead leaves and mud. The crab-eating frog can hold her breath for a long time—hopefully until the dog-faced water snake gives up waiting for her.

Last night for dinner, the crab-eating frog swallowed...

... a gossamer-winged butterfly flailing in the shallow water. To see what another gossamer-winged butterfly is up to, TURN TO PAGE 19.

... a weaver ant that fell into the water. To see what another weaver ant is up to, TURN TO PAGE 35.

... a scorpion mud lobster scooting through the mud. To see what another scorpion mud lobster is up to, TURN TO PAGE 32.

... a porcelain fiddler crab scuttling across the sand. To see what another porcelain fiddler crab is up to, TURN TO PAGE 51.

Frog Farms

Have you ever eaten frog legs? The sturdy, long legs of the crab-eating frog are valued for their meat. In fact, crab-eating frogs are often grown on frog farms. People raise and feed the frogs and then sell them for food, much like other farms might do with cattle or chickens.

LONG-TAILED MACAQUE

(Macaca fascicularis)

Boing! Boing! The long-tailed macaque bounces on the branch. He bares his teeth, pulling his ears and nose back. He screeches at the rival macaque troop in the next tree over. As the alpha male, or leader, it is his job to protect and defend his troop of macaques. These are *his* troop's food and trees!

The alpha male of the intruding troop screeches and bounces too. But he and his macaques are the ones who have strayed too far. They back off. Slowly, the first male starts to calm down as the intruders move back.

Behind the male macaque, the rest of his troop starts to swing down the tree. They're mostly females, babies, and a few younger males. They're not retreating, it's just getting late. As the sun gets lower in the sky, the troop heads to their sleeping tree. Here, they'll huddle together for the night to keep warm. It's safer here in the trees over the river. If a predator—a snake, lizard, or bird—threatens them in the night, they can simply drop to the water below and swim to safety. When the macaques wake in the morning, they'll head back out to look for leaves and food. And hopefully they won't run into the other macaque troop again.

Last night for dinner, the long-tailed macaque nibbled . . .

Monkey Pest

Long-tailed macaques are not endangered, but they are frequently hunted and killed. Some people hunt them for food. Others kill them out of frustration. Long-tailed macaques can make nuisances of themselves. Sometimes they dig through people's garbage for food. And sometimes they find people's crops are tasty, especially

. . . some leaves from a mangrove apple tree. To find out what mangrove apples are like, TURN TO PAGE 14.

. . . some weaver ants traveling along a branch. To find out what other weaver ants are up to, TURN TO PAGE 35.

. . . some leaves from an api api putih tree. To find out what api api putih trees are like, TURN TO PAGE 38.

. . . a gossamer-winged butterfly caterpillar found under a leaf. To find out what another gossamer-winged butterfly is up to, TURN TO PAGE 19.

. . . a porcelain fiddler crab scuttling through the mud at low tide. To find out what another porcelain fiddler crab is up to, TURN TO PAGE 51.

. . . some golden leatherferns. To find out what the golden leatherferns of the mangrove forest are like, TURN TO PAGE 24.

. . . a scorpion mud lobster scooting through the shallow water. To find out what another scorpion mud lobster is up to, TURN TO PAGE 32.

GREEN CAT SNAKE (*Boiga cyanea*)

The thin, long green cat snake twines through the branches of the mangrove apple tree in the dark. She gets her name from her eyes. Her pupils (the black part in the center of her eyes) are tall and narrow, like a cat's pupils in the light.

The snake slides down the trunk. She flicks her tongue out at the green heron nest she discovered in the crook of the tree. Where is the mother bird? Off hunting? Or maybe injured somewhere? Either way, these eggs are unguarded. The cat snake makes quick work of it. She stretches her black mouth wide and swallows an egg. Her body bulges as the egg slides down her throat.

Suddenly, the green heron flaps back to the nest. The heron pecks and claws at the snake. The snake is knocked off the branch, but she catches herself on the branch below. She slithers off, leaving the heron in peace. The cat snake is satisfied too. The egg was the perfect dinner.

Last night for dinner, the green cat snake swallowed . . .

. . . a saltwater crocodile egg.
The snake was knocked out of the tree and found this tasty treat on the ground. To see what a saltwater crocodile is up to, TURN TO PAGE 9.

. . . eggs from a dog-faced water snake. To see what a dog-faced water snake is up to, TURN TO PAGE 46.

. . . a common kingfisher egg stolen from its nest. To see what a common kingfisher is up to, TURN TO PAGE 48.

. . . a Malaysian giant turtle egg, uncovered by a leopard. To see what another Malaysian giant turtle is up to, TURN TO PAGE 16.

. . . a baby large flying fox, left behind by the colony. To see what a large flying fox is up to, TURN TO PAGE 17.

. . . an Indian monitor lizard that just crawled out of his egg. To see what another Indian monitor lizard is up to, TURN TO PAGE 43.

. . . a crab-eating frog that thought it was hidden from sight. To see what another crab-eating frog is up to, TURN TO PAGE 54.

GLOSSARY

adapted: changed habits or physical characteristics, allowing the plant or animal to better fit the environment

amphibians: animals that live on both land and in water

bacteria: tiny living things made up of only one cell

brackish: slightly salty

carnivore: an animal that eats other animals

colony: a group of plants or animals of one species that live together

decomposers: living things, such as insects or bacteria, that feed on dead plants and animals

endangered: in danger of dying out

erode: to wear away

extinct: no longer existing

food chain: a system in which energy moves from the sun to plants and to animals as each eats and is eaten

food web: many food chains linked together. Food webs show how plants, animals, and other living things are connected in a habitat.

habitat: the place where a plant or animal naturally lives and grows

larvas: the wormlike stage in an insect's life between the egg and adult forms

nocturnal: awake and active at night

nutrients: substances, especially in food, that help a plant or animal survive

pesticides: poisons that are used to get rid of unwanted insects

pheromones: a chemical produced by an animal that causes other animals in the same species to behave in a certain way

pollen: yellowish grains inside a flower that help make seeds

predators: animals that hunt and kill other animals for food

prey: an animal that is hunted for food by another animal

primary consumers: animals that eat plants

producers: living things, such as plants, that make their own food

scavenger: an animal that eats dead plants or animals

secondary consumers: animals and insects that eat other animals and insects

sediments: tiny pieces of rock and other matter that sink in liquids

species: a group of related animals or plants

spores: small seeds that can be used to grow new living things without reproduction

tertiary consumers: animals that eat other animals and have few natural enemies

venom: a poison made by an animal and injected into its prey

FURTHER READING AND WEBSITES

Animals
   http://animals.nationalgeographic.com
   Find your favorite mangrove animal in this comprehensive guide to animals around the world.

Blaxland, Beth. *Mangroves*. New York: Chelsea House, 2001. The mangrove habitat is explored with photographs and illustrations.

Chapman, Simon. *Explorers Wanted!: In Deepest Borneo*. Glasgow: Egmont Books, 2005. In this interactive adventure, you can explore the island of Borneo, where the mangrove forest in this book is set.

Cherry, Lynne. *The Sea, the Storm and the Mangrove Tangle*. New York: Farrar, Straus, and Giroux, 2004. Follow a hundred-year life cycle of a mangrove tree in this fictional story.

Guide to the Mangroves of Singapore
   http://mangrove.nus.edu.sg/guidebooks
   Discover more about mangrove forests in Singapore, near the island of Borneo.

Heinrichs, Ann. *Malaysia*. New York: Children's Press, 2005. This books discusses the country of Malaysia, including its people and its natural resources.

Silver, Donald M. *Swamp*. New York: McGraw-Hill, 1997. Swamps and wetlands around the world are introduced and examined.

SELECTED BIBLIOGRAPHY

Baker, Nick. *Ecology Asia*. 2008. http://www.ecologyasia.coma (November 28, 2008).

Borneo Coast: Creatures of the Mangrove. VHS. Washington, DC: National Geographic Society, 1997.

Bruce, Jenni, Karen McGhee, Luba Vangelova, and Richard Vogt. *The Encyclopedia of Animals: A Complete Visual Guide*. Berkeley: University of California Press, 2004.

Burnie, David, and Don E. Wilson. *Animal: The Definitive Visual Guide to the World's Wildlife*. London, New York: DK, 2005.

IUCN Species Survival Commission. "2007 IUCN Red List of Threatened Species." *IUCN*. N.d. http://www.iucnredlist.org/ (November 14, 2008).

McGinley, Mark, ed. "Sundra Shelf Mangroves." *Encyclopedia of Earth*. September 3, 2008. http://www.eoearth.org/article/Sunda_Shelf_mangroves (November 28, 2008).

PBS. "Borneo, Island in the Clouds, from Caves to Kinabalu." *pbs.org*. N.d. http://www.pbs.org/edens/borneo/mangrove.htm (November 28, 2008).

World Wildlife Fund. 2008. http://www.worldwildlife.org/home.html (November 14, 2008).

INDEX

Photo Acknowledgments

The images in this book are used with the permission of: © Tim Laman/
National Geographic/Getty Images, pp. 1, 4–5, 6–7, 9, 11, 13, 15, 23, 25, 26,
28, 31, 33, 37, 40, 45, 47, 49, 53, 55, 57, 59; © Bill Hauser/Independent Picture
Service, pp. 5, 38 (bottom); © Dr. Hisashi Matubayashi, p. 8; © Brandon Cole/
Visuals Unlimited/Getty Images, p. 10; © age fotostock/SuperStock, pp. 12, 50;
© Ria Tan/www.wildsingapore.com, pp. 14 (both), 24, 27, 38 (top), 39, 51;
© Arco Images GmbH/Alamy, p. 16; © Reinhard Dirscherl/Visuals Unlimited,
Inc., p. 17; © Thomas Marent/Minden Pictures, p. 18; © OSF/Mantis W.F./
Animals Animals, p. 19; © iStockphoto.com/tcp, p. 20; Courtesy KK Kuo/Birding
in Taiwan, pp. 21, 22 (top); © Pete Oxford/naturepl.com, p. 22 (bottom);
AP Photo/WWF, Alain Compost, HO, p. 29; © Thomas Kitchin & Victoria Hurst/
First Light/Alamy, p. 30; © ANT Photo Library/Photo Researchers, p. 32; © Hans
Christian Heap/Taxi/Getty Images, p. 35; © PREMAPHOTOS/naturepl.com, p. 36;
© David Doubilet/National Geographic/Getty Images, p. 41; © Kim Taylor/
naturepl.com, p. 42; © Daniel Heuclin/NHPA/Photoshot, pp. 43, 58 (top);
© Gary Neil Corbett/SuperStock, p. 44; © Gregory Guida/Natural Visions, p. 46;
© Fritz Polking/Visuals Unlimited, Inc., p. 48; © Jane Burton/naturepl.com,
p. 52; © Alessandro Mancini/Alamy, p. 54; © Martin Harvey/The Image Bank/
Getty Images, p. 56; © David A. Northcott/CORBIS, p. 58 (bottom).
Illustrations for game board and pieces © Bill Hauser/Independent Picture
Service.

Front Cover: © Tim Laman/National Geographic/Getty Images (background,
second from left, and right); © iStockphoto.com/Erik Rumbaugh (left); © David
Doubilet/National Geographic/Getty Images (second from right).

About the Authors

Don Wojahn and Becky Wojahn are school library media specialists by day and
writers by night. Their natural habitat is the temperate forests of northwestern
Wisconsin, where they share their den with two animal-loving sons and two big
black dogs. The Wojahns are the authors of all twelve books in the Follow that
Food Chain series.